RHYME AND REASON

THE TRANSIENT

*Observations of
and Reflections on
Nature*

By Josephine M. Woods

a Kiwi in Yorkshire

First published in Great Britain as a softback original in 2014

Copyright © 2014 Josephine M Woods

The moral right of this author has been asserted.

Typeset in Baskerville and Baskerville Old Face

Editing, design and publishing by UK Book Publishing

UK Book Publishing is a trading name of Consilience Media

www.ukbookpublishing.com

ISBN: 978-1-910223-15-4

REORDER – if not available through retail outlets please contact Josephine – josephine.m.woods@gmail.com

Contents

Acknowledgments

To

Our kindly neighbours, past and present, of Corn Mill;

Our Philosophy brothers and sisters;

Our family and friends who have been so supportive;

Especially my patient and enthusiastic husband Robert who
has worked so hard to prepare this book for its publishing;

My dear old Dad whose love of poetry and
children's stories has inspired me;

The flora and fauna, seasons and weather of the Yorkshire countryside;

And lastly to the Muse of Poetry who has allowed
these verses to come so easily to mind.

The authoress is just the scribe.

Introduction

In May 2010 a New Zealand retired Primary School teacher and her husband moved to live in Corn Mill, a quiet cul-de-sac on the outskirts of Menston, a small village some 12 miles north west of Leeds.

Facing east and nestled at the bottom of the western flank of the Chevin Hill, the flora, fauna, wildlife and seasons provide the setting for 'A Kiwi in Yorkshire's Observations Of and Reflections On Nature'

Since arriving in the UK in 2005 – first to Scotland then Yorkshire – she has written several other series of books: picture books for younger children; fantasy series for girls; adventure space series for boys and an illustrated series of stories of New Zealand birds.

This first anthology of The Transient will be followed by a sequel called The Eternal.

e-books and print are being considered for publishing.

Praise

To praise the glory of the Universe,
It is so natural to the human soul,
For in the glory of this Universe
We see the pattern of the whole.
This glory, it expands our aching heart,
Dissolves all sorrow and from there we start
To see that heaven, it is here on Earth.
We can enjoy, we can join in its mirth
And this is why we have a human birth.

After the Rain

The garden feels so fresh after the rain.
The flora drink it gleefully, their life force to sustain.
The scents are rich and sweet and smell of earth.
The seedlings spring forth joyfully
Increasing height and girth.

The air is cool and with each breath one's being fills with peace
And with each breath one feels the power of energy increase.
The raindrops sit like jewels upon each flower and on each leaf.
The rain has blessed this garden and one feels its great relief.
Enjoying every moment one remembers - life is brief.

They say God is in a garden with its peace, its quiet repose.
In every tree, in every shrub, in every scented rose.
Let us dwell there in our autumn years
As life's book starts to close.

Black Cat

Black Cat on silent paws
Like a shadow slinks into the meadow
The dormice stop and listen.
They hear not a rustle.

Then she strikes!
They all squeal in fright,
Then scatter!
Their peace is shattered
And one of them breathes no more.

Black Cat on silent paws
Like a shadow slinks out of the meadow
And by the cottage door
A gift she leaves,
The mouse that lives no more.

Autumn

The trees they start to go to sleep,
Their sap drawn down
Through Earth's dark deep.

Their leaves, they start to die.
On winds they whirl down
To the ground to lie
And slowly melt away
And turn again to clay.

The pot that's formed of clay returns,
Just as our heart for Him it yearns
When it's our end of day.

From earth to earth.
From dust to dust.
From clay pot back to clay.

Beauty

It's such a pity
That the beauty of a rose
Must fade away
And drop its satin petals
At its close of day.

All lovely things
They bud and bloom and die,
Surrendering their glory
To the earth beneath God's sky.

Yet all our beauties past
And present never fade,
As in our memories'

Protective shade
They live eternally
And as <u>we</u> never die,
They'll always live,
In each of us abide
And never end.

Dead Bird

Dead Bird,
So beautiful in repose.
Did that foe like night
Strike you down in flight
As you from the garden rose?

Dead Bird,
So serene and still.
Does your soul fly in the air
Though your form is lying here?
Do you sing at the gates of dawn
To welcome in the morn,
Free to roam at will?
Dead Bird,
So serene and still.

Devoted Parents

There is a high pitched chirruping in the nest.
The starling parents working with such zest
As back and forth they fly the whole day long,
No time to sing their starling's joyful song.

I used to sit here in the early spring
And he'd puff out his chest and to me sing.
Then I would try to mimic all his whistles sweet and clicking tweets
But he'd outdo my human muted cheeps.

Now back and forth with insects, worms and beetles they fly fast
And offer to their chicks this rich repast.
Life's such a feeding frenzy for these two.
Their duty human parents can't outdo
As each few seconds they arrive out of the blue
To feed this hungry throng.
It's back and forth and back the whole day long
till finally the sun sinks in the west
And these exhausted parents
Have earnt a short night's rest.

Cock Pheasant on Chevin's Pastures Green

Cock Pheasant streaks across
the grassy green.
His rustic feathers glowing
With a glorious sun rayed sheen.
He is so fearful yet
So dignified and proud
As suddenly he disappears
'neath leafy shadow's shroud.

He far outshines his mistress
With her drab and motley gown
That camouflages her so well
In grass and brambles brown.

I hear him cockle valiantly
From safety in leaf's shade.
He drums the ground
With feisty dance
That rumbles through the glade.

But when his brood
They venture forth
Too far on open ground,
He runs along in hot pursuit
With fervent glance all round.

To protect them!
That's his duty!
He would fight till death
One feels
With any wandering predator that
Towards them quietly steals.

Escorting them back safe and sound
Inside his territory,
The king of all this green terrain
And dappled brood he'll be
Until –
A younger pheasant comes –
Defeating him –
And of his worldly duty
Sets him free.

Evening Light

I love the golden sunlight
As it shines on Chevin's green
And teases out the shadows
Across this blessed scene.

The house up there upon the hill,
It basks in its own majesty
As evening's spotlight glorifies
Each window that I see.

The softness – so enchanting,
I wish it long would stay.
So briefly one's heart captures it
Before the end of day
Descends into the dusky night
And shadows slowly fade away.

So till tomorrow's evening when
We just may see the scene again,
But come what may
We do not know
What English weather will hold sway
And what new glory
It may bring
To days so fickle
In the spring.

Grey Squirrel

Grey squirrel flits across the grass –
Then stops –
Then flicks his tail.
He glances round, then dashes on,
His tail like dusky sail.

His form it flows o'er green
Like waves on undulating sea
That run to shore before the wind,
Then – scampering up a tree
He leaps and dips and dives
As from branch to branch he skives.

When he stops his acrobatics
He sits hunched in monkey pose.
From tiny hands he nibbles nuts
Then off again he goes
From branch to branch
And tree to tree,
Then into bushes green
He disappears;
A ripple on that leafy scene
Is all that shows
The trail where he has been.

Heaven in a Garden

There's joy in a garden
Where bees buzz and hum.
There's joy in a garden
Where flowers face the sun.

There's joy in a garden
Where to sit is pure bliss,
Where there's warmth and sweet perfume
And bright sunshine's kiss.

There's joy in a garden
Where the warm smell of earth
Reminds one of heaven
Whence we took our birth.

The shrubs and the trees
And the warm summer breeze,
The song of the birds in the sky.
The space and the air
That plays in one's hair;
No wonder one lets out a sigh.

O forever to stay in this garden
Would be heaven for here we can play
As the fairies and sprites
Through the warm summer nights.
What bliss for our soul here to stay
As we come near the end of our day.

O Bullfinch Proud

O Bullfinch with your paunch so red
With silver back and jet black head
There sitting in the cherry tree
You peck away and peer at me.

I – like a giant bird
Here sitting in my lair
All snug and warm and still
In my big cosy chair
Is that what you think
As you peck and stare?

So dignified and portly
That proud and puffed up chest.
It looks much more magnificent
Than Robin's dusky breast.

A master of your territory
Imperiously you stare at me
Just like a stately king
Then, with a flick of your proud tail,
Away you flit – so swiftly on the wing.

Summer's Zenith Past

No longer birdsong fills the air,
Their joy ecstatic no more rings
From heaven to Earth and all around
And to my soul their silence brings
A sadness that the summer's peak
Is once again on the retreat
Towards the lessening of the light,
To lesser day and longer night.

But with the nesting frenzy gone
What need is there for fervent song?
The brood has grown and now it's flown
To start new life in yonder glade,
Amongst its leafy shade.

And so the sunset sooner comes
And takes us towards autumn's rest.
The summer days are quieter now
As our babes too have flown the nest.
'Tis time to stop and contemplate,
To rest and then to meditate
On lessons that we've had to learn
And all negation we must spurn
Then fill our hearts with love.
Take guidance from above
And as we reach our journey's end
Just hope our soul to Him ascends
With Him to find repose.
Extinguishing all woes.

Winter Silence

As I gaze o'er my window sill
And see those houses standing still.
The cherry tree that hardly moves,
The grey sky up above the rooves
And aerials and chimney pots.
The world this time of year it stops,
Or so it seems.

A tiny breeze in the cherry tree
Shimmers the leaves now yellow.
Wee birds silently zipping by,
The atmosphere so mellow.

Is this the calm before the storm?
An arctic blast will soon descend.
That's what the weatherman did say,
I listened to him yesterday.
So we inside must stay
And keep ourselves all toasty warm.

But now, in silence all abides.
The trees have gone to sleep.
Their sap withdrawn from every twig
Into the dark earth deep.

Is that a snow cloud that I spy
In ominously loaded sky?
Oh well, the winter it looms near,
With silence then comes peace and rest.
With silence we are blest.

Snow Flakes

Down the tiny snowflakes fall
Like cherry blossom floating on the breeze.

Hypnotic

Microscopic

Silent

So serene.
I gaze in wonder at this snowy scene.

Just like the glass dome
So fascinating to my childlike gaze
That winter scene to shake
And watch those snowflakes through the glaze
Descend and settle in this glass dome's dream.

Now are we like that tiny play
Within a dome,
In yet a bigger dream?

Does God look down from skies above,
Around us, through and through
Upon this play he's made for us,
Just watching me and you?

Rabbits in the Snow

Rabbits frolic in the snow
Dashing, pausing, digging down below.

Hopping, stopping
Ears up straight
Glancing round for fox in wait
Or cat or dog or bird of prey
That glides above
'neath clouds of grey.

Dashing round and off they race
Each one taking turns to chase.
Again they stop and have a nuzzle
Which boy, which girl?
Now there's a puzzle

Then off to sleep beneath the tree
In burrow deep where we can't see.
A grassy nest for cosy rest
With tiny babies suckling at each breast.

Our Boy on the Hunt

The Boy is on the hunt again,
In evening's light in yonder field.
One wonders what his wanderings
Upon this night will yield.

Will it be a large brown rat
Or baby rabbit round and fat?
Our neighbour says she's found a skull
Beneath her shrubbery.
I shudder at the thought of it.
What creature's could it be?
I do not want to see.

I do not wish to know
What antics he's been up to in the night
When in he comes so loveable
And cute in morning's light.

Snowy Yorkshire

Grey days depart and here's the snow,
It brings us such delight.
It brightens up the winter days,
A glistening, heartening sight.

The cars drive carefully o'er the hill
With white toupees of snow.
The sun shines on the silent fields
And lends a golden glow.

The snowflakes cascade down again
So gently after driving rain.
The wind and floods we soon forget,
The dry snow halting damp and wet
Until that time when comes the thaw
And rain it then descends once more.

But while the snowflakes swirl around
And gently cloak the sleeping ground
And dresses pines with snowy frills
And ices flower pots, window sills
And lamp-posts in the street.

We'll for a time forget the rain and sleet.

A Snowy Scene

The stage is set –
A snow clad scene
On Being's changeless unseen screen.

The beauty of each tree is blest
By snowflakes as they come to rest
On conifers green
And hawthorns bare
Of leaves and berries
That hung there
In days of rain before the snow
Those ornaments that once did grow
When spring showed at its best.

But for now those trees
In winter's silence stand
With dignity, dressed in their white cloak,
The maples and the sturdy oak.

The conifers like Christmas trees
All frosted by an icy breeze
That blows the snowflakes
Gently o'er their gown,
As soft and light as feather eiderdown.

A diamond cluster tumbles from a branch
And cascades down –
A tiny avalanche.

Each stake around the raspberry canes
Looks like a lollypop
With balls of snow on top.

Flower pots that on the patio stand
With crowns of icing look so grand,
Like giant cupcakes
Standing in a row
Welcome yet more snow.

And as one gazes at the scene
That's so surreal and so serene
The purity of Being shows

As on and on it snows.

Icicles

Star shaped diamonds dress the window pane,
Then melt to drops and run down like the rain
Onto the sill beneath,
Then to the earth bequeath
Their moisture yet again.

Icicles begin to grow
Beneath a white halo of snow
And from each tip
Melts drip drip drip
Each drop to merge
With pools soon formed below.

Those geometric starry shapes
That nature it so cleverly makes,
How does that pattern form?
From what intelligence is it born
And built so thus to grow
Into each individual shape?

How will we ever know
That godly geometric mind
Which forms all creatures so?

Not one is like the other,
Each from its own seed's heart
Is formed and grows from essence
From that plan each will start,
To grow and to develop
Its uniqueness to impart
The glory of this universe.

Oh humans just how smart are we,
Can we create such forms
From such an unseen cause?
It makes us stop and think - then we take pause.

We too were formed in such a way
This we forget from day to day
But when remembered,
Then our heart again to heaven soars
To dwell in quiet humility at heaven's doors.

The Sun's Return

How good to see the sun again
When snow and ice and sleet and rain
Have finally departed.
The spring at last has started
To peep above the Earth.

The crocuses and snowdrops
Then tulips, daffodils
Are showing forth their glory,
Their colours and their frills.

How good to see the sun again
There glistening through the window pane.
It lights the heart
And warms the head
And heals our darkened eyes
To gaze on brighter skies.

How long one wonders will it stay?
The hours they lengthen day by day,
But will the big chill stay away?
I certainly hope it will.

Rainbows

The world is but a rainbow,
Here today, gone tomorrow.
Ever changing,
Rearranging elemental
Forms and colours.
Shades and shadows
Chase each other.
On a merry dance they lead us
Round and round through lives
They feed us
With their fantasies and woes.
On and on each of us goes
From the womb towards the grave,
Each life just like an ocean wave
Into the silent depths descends
And so all lives come to their ends
In universal sleep
These forms they merge – into its cradle deep.

Sparrow Hawk

Sparrow Hawk! O menace!
Swooping down low o'er the grass.
Your shadow hovers like a ghost
As o'er the sun you pass.

A cawing rook takes flight and flees
As you give chase
He dives and turns
His flight towards the trees.

Then up you soar
To heights once more,
Then search with fiercesome eyes
For any movement on the ground,
As well as in the sky.

O Sparrow Hawk!
As hunger burns
Why blame you
When attention turns
Again towards the hunt.
You give such fascinating joy
With each new aerial stunt.

As on the thermals up you ride,
We watch you swoop,
We watch you glide.
Then into sunset's orange glow,
Your silhouette it melts away.
So home to roost
In some lone nest to sleep,
Then hunt another day.

Sunflower

O sunflower – solar representative on Earth
Whose mentor shines above,
That lends his nature, form and light
To you to show his love.

O sunflower – tall and dignified,
We look into your face.
Your seeds will sow a thousand suns
This earthly world to grace.

O sunflower – as your petals wilt,
As your day turns to night,
Your seeds they feed the birds and mice
As your soul takes its flight.

O sunflower – once again you shine,
Your soul has joined the sun
And in the day you soar above,
As sun and flower are one.

Dedicated to Bruce Robinson,
lover of sunflowers.

Tall Tree

Tall tree on yonder hill
Standing proud against the sky.
Your stillness hardly ruffled
By the wind that passes by.

The cows they wander quietly in your shade,
Their heads bowed down in reverence
For the grass they love to graze.

Oblivious are they of you reaching for the sky.
Your green form soaring heavenwards
My heart it does inspire
To raise my sight from pastures green
Towards that heavenly light
And offer up my arms
To praise God's glory and His might.

The Bats!

There go the bats!
Small phantoms of the twilight zone
They zip and zigzag through the dusk
On prey their sensors finely honed.

There go the bats!
Into the forest dark they melt
Like shadows, on the hunt
Beware small creatures of the night
Beware their fatal bite.

Here come the bats!
As dawn's dim glow begins to show
Across a cloudless sky
Here back they come now
One by one
Towards their lair they fly.

Where do they come from every night?
Where do they sleep all day?
Yet every night at summer's height
When sun and birds have gone to bed
Into the forest's depth again
On silent wings they head.

The Curlew's Cry

The Curlews are calling
Way up on the hill
On a warm Sunday morning
So peaceful and still.

Their call is so plaintive
On dew laden air
One wonders, "what could they be
Doing up there?"

"How long till they fly
To their new winter home?"
One wonders, "How far
O'er the world do they roam?"

For now it is autumn,
Their babies all grown
From their nests in green pastures
They've already flown.

And as the days shorten
Their wings will grow strong,
For the journey they'll fly on
Is hard and so long.

One wishes them well
On their forthcoming flight,
For life is a journey
From darkness to light.

Our journey, like theirs
Is dark and unknown.
Our future uncertain,
To us it's not shown.

Each day we awaken
To pleasure and pain.
Until we find peace,
And then it is plain.
Our needs are all met.
There is no more to gain.

And so like the curlews
Up there on the hill,
We dwell in God's presence,
So peaceful and still.

The Cherry Tree

The cherry tree is dancing in the summer breeze
Adorned with leaves of green.
Its fruit peeps through
Like tiny orbs of jade,
They hang and bob and sway,
Awaiting summer's warming kiss
From dawn of day.

I see a pigeon land and sink and disappear
Among that greenery moving like a glistening sea
Then out among its foliage peeps a Pied Coal Tit
That cocks its head to one side as it looks at me.

Then upward from the leafy sea,
Just like a phoenix soars
That pigeon, breast puffed out and wings held wide,
So like an angel rising up through clouds on every side.
Then over roof tops once again I see him glide.

The tree again sways gently in the summer breeze,
Its shiny leaves reflect the summer sun
Until the storms of autumn blow them all away.
The tree then goes to sleep – its job is done.

The Doe

I saw a doe this morning
In yonder field at early light.
She ran across on slender legs,
Her gait so graceful
In her flight.

Her white rump flashed
Her presence
As she dashed away,
Then leapt over
The wall of stones,
She did not want to stay.

Yet other times I've seen her,
Then she's been quite at ease.
Content to graze
'Midst bramble camouflage
And hawthorn trees.

She glances round,
Her shapely large soft ears
They capture every tiny
Sound she hears.

She doesn't mind me
And my silent gaze,
As quietly she continues
There to graze
And wander at her will,
In dawn's soft golden sunlight
Warm and still.

The Heron's Flight

Today I watched the heron's sombre flight
With legs outstretched against the grey cloud's light

His head sits ponderously on his outthrust chest.
His wing strokes slow as onwards towards destination's rest
He goes,
To wade in water of some distant lake,
His measured steps to find a fish he'll take
Among tall reeds and grasses
- Stopping there –
Just like a statue –
Frozen in the air!

His eyes unblinking:
Neck and beak in wait
To strike his catch.
He strikes!
His beak now full of bait,
In several gulps his hunger he doth sate.

He shows such patience
And determination
Steadfast in his solitary state.
We too should learn such patience
And to wait
Until God shows to us
Our pre-determined fate.

The Magnolia Tree

On yon magnolia tree
Some buds they have unfurled
While others as yet they remain uncurled.
The branches sway and hold up in the evening breeze
These blooms like yachts in a regatta
Tossed on stormy seas.

The lichen covered branches
Display their blooms up high
As grey clouds barrel eastwards
Blotting out blue sky.

One hopes the frost will stay away
And leave unblemished with brown blot
These white and pink silk flowers
And may they stay unsullied
By strong winds and April showers.

The sight of these pale branches so festooned
Brings joy releasing one from winter's gloom
Unto grey days they bring such sweet delight
Their beauty so assuages winter's blight
That dulls the mind,
They're such a cheerful sight.

And when they're done
Those satin petals fall upon the earth
And carpet it about their tree trunk's girth
Then other flowers bloom and take their turn
To spread spring's gaiety with rich rebirth.

The First Bumble Bee

I saw a great big bumble bee
Sitting on a wall.
He's been sleeping all through winter
Since last year in the Fall.

He sat shivering in the sun
On this fresh spring sunny morn.
He looked so weak and hungry
And also quite forlorn.

He whirred his wings to try them
And to dry them in the sun.
To sleep for six months through the winter storms
Can't be much fun.

I went to get some honey from its jar
And smeared it on the ledge not very far
From where he sat so furry black and yellow
And so fat.

I watched him move towards it
And then what did I see?
His long proboscis sticking out
And sucking that honey.

He sucked about a minute
And then he had a rest.
He sucked some more
So then, more full of zest,
He whirred his tiny wings
Then flew into sunlight.
That honey gave him energy
To start upon his flight.

I hoped the blossom on the cherry tree
Would soon come out to feed this bumble bee
And many other bumble bees besides,
As through the daffodils and snowdrops they will glide.

I wonder if he'll come back
To the honey on the wall?
There may not be too many flowers yet
To feed them all.

But every year this play it does occur.
So bumble bee, good luck to you
As on those wings
You hum and buzz and whirr
Through gardens just awakening to spring,
With shooting bulbs and blossoms
And nesting birds that sing
So full of joy to see and feel the sun.
Awaiting all the sunnier, warmer,
Longer days to come.

The Moon's Glow

The Moon's glow emanates
Through shrouds,
Those chiffon wisps
Of blue grey clouds.

Below – those shadows of the night
They dimly form
In its cool light
the houses, trees and fields and walls,
on these dark forms the moon's light falls.

Then it is gone,
As cloud's dark hue
Removes all trace of our moon's view.

And so mind's clouds
From our soul's sight
They dim our view
Of our own light.

How do we chase these clouds away
And from that light no longer stray.
How can we in that presence stay
And live in peace
Each moment of each day?

The Wren's Warning

Wee Wren cries his warning
Chit! Chit! Chit!
I can see that cat
So beware of it.

We don't want him near
Our precious nest.
We need to protect
Our eggs where they rest.

The black and white cat
On silent paws
Departs then to rest
On his bed indoors.

Two Ducks

"Quack! Quack! Quack! Come back, come back, come back!"

So in the dawn on a Sunday morn
Two ducks fly round and round.

And as the clouds, they roll on by,
So on and on the two ducks fly.

"Some eggs for ducklings we must make,"
So on and on he quacks, that drake.

When will he coax her to the ground,
To find a nest that's safe and sound
To hatch those ducklings in?

They first must mate, it's getting late,
Consent he must first win!

So as those clouds keep rolling by
And it begins to rain.
Round and past that pair they fly
Again, again, again.

They beat the air with fervent wings
As all the other birds they sing.
Their chorus round the valley rings,
Such joy to we who hear it brings.

The nesting spree, it has begun.
The starlings, busy in the sun
With bits of straw fly forth and back,
They are so full of zest.

But those two ducks still fly and quack
And so the play, it shall proceed
Until again at summer's end
At last, all comes to rest.

We Need a Little Garden

We need a little garden
Warm and peaceful,
That is sheltered from the wind
But not the sun.
With sweetly climbing roses
And wisteria.
Where sweet peas waft
Their scent to everyone.

We would have a little seat
Among the flower beds,
With a rosemary bush
And lavender or two.
There would be a small sundial
Who at the sun would smile
And cast its morning shadow
O'er the dew.

We need a little garden
Warm and peaceful,
With hollyhocks and foxgloves
By the wall.
With hyacinths pink and blue
And lobelia peeping through.
With a cherry tree
Whose blossoms we'd watch fall.

We would have a little fountain
In a corner,
With a tiny bubbling brook (beck)
And waterfall.
We would sit there by the pool
In the shadow where it's cool,
While the curlews
Serenade us with their call.

And as the evening shadows
Start to lengthen,
In the evening of our life
As old age creeps.
So there quietly time goes by
And with a final sigh
We may slip into that
Vast eternal sleep.

Wild Horses

Grey clouds race across the sky,
Wild horses on a distant plain.
These horses, though, like ghosts they change their shape
As seconds pass they never stay the same.

Then finally they disappear up over yonder hill.
Behind there comes a sea of cloud,
With this the sky begins to fill.

No more the shapes of beasts or birds.
No, none of them remain.
But just the cloudy sea and wind
Soon followed by the rain.

And so the phases of our lives
Take shape, then change, then disappear
Into that sea of time passed by.
They, like the clouds there in the sky,
Will never reappear.

So life moves on through wind and rain
And then the sun comes out again
And frees us from all fear.
That cloud that dims our heart and mind
Of that our soul it finally will clear.

Willow seeds

The air is full of willow seeds,
Like teeny tiny tumbleweeds.
I see them floating in the air,
So dandelions you must beware.
So many of them are out there
And where they land they do not care.

They far outnumber all of you,
As clouds of them float in the blue
And each can grow into a tree
To overshadow you and me.

Then when the sun appears in May
Again these clouds of seeds will stray
On gentle breezes through each day.
Till each one finds its earthly rest,
Wherever it may grow the best,
Then forth will spring another tree
To overshadow you and me.

The Pigeons

Coo COOO COOO coo COOO
Coo COOO COOO coo COOO
Coo COOO COOO coo COOO
- coo!

So he pursues her.
He'll coo and whoo her
Until his timely death!

They'll fly and flutter,
Each coo he'll utter
Until his final breath!

This ardent lover,
His mate he'll cover,
With fond and passionate peck!

He'll chase and love her
He'll smooch and smother
With lust her downy neck!

When wooing's over
She'll head for cover
In pine tree's hidden nest.

Those eggs she'll lay there,
Then he'll protect her
From every bird and pest.

When fledglings leave them
This play proceeds then
And we'll perceive his zest
Again COOO coo COOO
Coo COOO COOO coo COOO
Coo COOO COOO coo COOO
- coo!

When will he ever rest?

An Aerial Dogfight Over The Chevin

An aerial dogfight it takes place
O'er Chevin's green and brambling, stony wall.
I sit and watch it silently
As it unfolds and so enthrals.

A sparrowhawk is soaring near
This valley lined with trees and brambles green.
Two crows fly forth to guard their flock
Into this spacious scene.
With threatening cause they dive upon their foe,
Though they are half as large as he,
In hot pursuit they go.

The hawk cries out as each crow strikes
To drive him hence.
He swoops and soars and circles round,
From them there's no defence.

The crows' attack, it perseveres
Until the hawk has flown o'er yonder hill.
They circle round to see him off,
As slowly, now, he disappears.

Then back they fly content their young and
Lady crows are safe and sound,
Not knowing that the other birds
Are also safe that live in trees all round.

This valley, that's so rich
In birdsong every day.
This saga have I seen unfold
So many times this May.

So May days linger on till start of June's
And fledgling starlings, pigeons, blackbirds,
Wrens sing forth their tunes
They echo up and down this valley deep
From early dawn to evening late
When finally all this drama stops
All then finally fall asleep.

Protected daily by the vigilant crow
And where the sparrowhawk now sleeps
We'll never know.

The Fox

A fox all rusty red
With sharp and hungry face
Lopes out upon the meadow
Right towards the place
Where frightened prey,
A rabbit, huddles in the grass
In hope the fox won't smell him
And soon will swiftly pass.

The fox, she leaps up high
With heavy pounce;
This rabbit will no longer
hop and bounce.

Then off across the field
The fox she goes
Towards her den
With this day's meal
Where cubs may wait
To welcome her with
Yelps and squeals.

This tenuous hold on life
Each day this type of drama
It reveals.

For life is short for all
So catch the moment of the 'Now'.
As to that fate we must relent
And meet with graceful bow.

Future

Do I yearn to live again in distant climes,
In bright New Zealand where I grew
And lived more youthful times?

The weather here in sullen England can defeat the soul,
But when in spring the glory doth unfold,
The joy, it elevates the heart
And depths of winter so soon doth depart.

The daffodil's blossom bursts upon the scene.
The leaf buds on grey skeletons of branches can be seen
To give a promise of bright days to come,
Of barbecues in evenings full of sun.

I wonder, do I wish to leave these pastures green?
The will of God as yet has not been seen.
I only know what's now and what has been.
I wait for guidance – in time – this He'll give
And we will know the country
Where in future we will live.

Poetry's Muse

Poetry is a song of praise,
It comes to one on Muse's wings.
The words take form in quiet mind
And to our heart it sings.

The mystery of this Muse evades enquiry by the mind,
But in our heart it sows its seed
Beyond all thought its soul we find
And there rejoice,
A scribe is all we are
To Muse's voice.

Future Publications

VERSE

Rhyme and Reason – The Eternal – *Sequel to The Transient*

CHILDREN'S PICTURE BOOK AND SHORT STORIES

Bessy Bumble Bee – Picture Book series (7-9 yrs)

The stories of Bessy, a baby bumble bee, meeting and having adventures with the creatures of the English countryside.

Contains first principles for reading and writing in a fun way.

Phoebe: fantasy series for young girls (9-15 yrs)

A young girl goes to sleep and enters a fantasy world.

Based on Josephine's favourite poetry.

Burt the Bionic Bogey series for boys (6-9 yrs)

Story of a young Martian, Burt and his Earth friend, Sam and their adventures around the universe in Burt's rocket space car.

Kepa the Kiwi (7-9 yrs)

Illustrations capturing the colour and character of the birds.

Kepa a young kiwi goes on adventures with the other birds in the New Zealand ancient forests before humans arrived.